THE BREEZE

NEESHANT SRIVASTAVA

Made with ♥ on the Notion Press Platform
www.notionpress.com

To the survival of man.

Contents

Contents

Contents

1. DREAM

A dream never dreamt is a dream fulfilled,
What is then my dream,
Perhaps happiness in those eyes,
That dreamt of me that I did not know,
Those eyes are long gone,
Into the mist of another world,
Leaving me unsure of my dream,
Yes, I do have a dream, I cannot lie,
But its too distant to even think about it,
My neck is at the blade of a sword,
I have heard of justice, albeit late,
And those passing eyes would have yearned for it,
Perhaps more than me for their own sake,
And for the defamed family name,
I would if I could and I am not complaining,
For the wheels are finally spinning,
They say one has to be lost to be found,
And I have been lost for ages now,
When others have come to a firm conclusion,
That my family died with my father's name,
And the rest have morphed into lifeless,
Let's dream a dream,
And see what it brings.

2. BIRDS HAVE FLOWN

What the father had for his children,
Was nothing more than a patch of green,
And sparkling sun rays from the east and west,
An open view for the little birds and squirrels,
Peaceful winds that spoke so softly,
A place of rest when the legs did tire,
Rooms that were quiet and pensive,
Protecting their sons and daughters from danger,
A wooden dining table to sit around for supper,
Rooms with windows for the breeze of the skies,
If heaven does exist,
Then it is here in my grandfather's abode,
Where the birds have all flown except for one,
Missing the greatest gift of humanity,
That the forefathers gave their children,
The hand of sweet blessing.

3. SELF MADE

What did you make of yourself,
Before you proclaim to be self-made,
Bags of gold over your shoulders,
When the fight began with a penny in the pocket,
You let that penny grow into an evergreen tree,
For posterity and your dear ones,
Man at its essence needs to be created,
To be moulded and shaped like at the hands of a potter,
With sharp instruments like the chisel and the hammer,
To be beaten heartlessly and repeatedly in the heat of the hearth,
The true self is far and unimaginable,
Blocked by the deeds of the past and the black dough of sins,
That weigh heavy on the shoulders and the soul,
To win a bag of money is to be a dissatisfied heart,
The challenge is far too fierce than can be thought,
And when something beautiful is created,
It is fragrant as a flower and melodious as a sublime song,
Every part of the human then is a feast for the eyes,
Heaven is just a knock away,
The mind symphony is the music of silence,
Then we have truly made the self,
And must be given due credit,
Lives flow like a river endlessly,
It's for us to wet the clay and create something.

4. WHERE IS INDIA

This is age of Indian Diaspora,
America has taken over an entire civilization,
The American way is the brains of a few,
While the rest have been de-wired dysfunctional,
It has hit the Indian shores and the young cannot think,
And someone else is tapping into our lost civilization,
To find clues to plunder if enough is still not enough,
Children on burgers and French fires and a smack of Italian,
Will not damage the upper tier,
Yet something is eating into their natural aptitude and thought,
Gone are those Gurukul days,
When boys and girls were kept miles apart,
Why is the world such a silent and dreary place,
Why do we only hear the sound of car wheels and honks,
Why are we not sure of our steps anymore,
Why is death a national issue,
And fear written on everyone's eyes,
Talk of an Indian renaissance,
Like the Romans,
Maybe we will follow the same cycle.

5. FATHERS AND SONS

O! father what did you earn,
Sons up the high ladder of echelon,
For the broad shoulder poverty in your walk,
By the busy market with your thumb a disgrace,
Your place of rest is still that nook of filth,
For you did not accept a penny from the worthy,
Three sons and the pride of the district,
You carried glasses of overflowing milk,
For miles in a starved stomach,
For your children conversing with Plato,
You sold your pride, your dreams for three geniuses,
And now each one has an abode,
While you hide from reality,
Their women won't let a sick man in,
When is a child worthy to be a son,
And you hone softeners for the rest of your life,
You gave up of yourself at your father's knees,
Deep in the village your eyes never dried,
You could never know the sorrow in your father's eyes,
Your father pushed you away to the city,
And entered a different world,
While the three great men ruled forever.

6. PASSING THOUGHT

I never knew what a dream is,
For I have never dreamt,
For dreamers are led to a common day,
Where the crowd converges to hear them,
And then shot dead in the heat of the day,
That does not mean that I am too cowardly,
To dare to have a dream,
Or that death is a stranger to me,
My words have nothing to win or lose,
My work is not my own,
My name never existed,
My life is a grace of God,
I thank him for making me human,
He has bestowed on me the present moment,
That is all I ever hope for,
The birds on the ledges and the leaves on trees,
Like spring between summer and winter,
Is enough for a quiet day, tranquil and peaceful,
My thoughts like the still water of a lake,
Carrying the brightness of skies in its womb,
Is this the right age to be born,
Where the war is on,
Everyone is hurt,
In a reckless race for an upper voice,
With lethal guns of conceit,

That hamper the delicate whiff of a passing breeze,
I do not dream anymore,
In my last leg to the warmth of my home.

7. AND DARKNESS FELL

I walked this road of dark,
Which made me forget my own existence,
I forgot my father and my home,
My youth groped for some touch,
I forgot the hardworking man,
Trying to catch the worms of meditation,
I forgot everything but my responsibilities,
Like an involuntary muscle it was unceasing,
I crossed the carnival for some other day,
Not knowing what I had lost,
My friends with hopeful eyes,
Often asked me of my victories,
Of twirls of fragrant hair over white temples,
And like a sick man I lied,
There is no end to this darkness, my friend,
What we call a dream is just a common goal,
Passed on by other such people sulking in darkness,
Or enjoying the privacy of it,
Where body games are a perfect amusement,
And the colours of the skin mingle into one,
And we just dive into euphoria,
Which is a replica of heaven,
If eyes ever open,
Then dreams are a reality,
And life is what is clear before our eyes,

And not some preconceived perception.

8. FINALLY, A DREAM

As a child I was asked,
What I wanted to be,
Like my wishes would take off,
High into the sky with wings,
And return with the gift I desired,
But I was quiet, like a shy six-year-old,
Only if I knew what my dreams were,
I looked into the eyes of my parents,
My father, a struggling man and quite unhappy,
My mother running around the house,
Tossing the corner of her sari over her shoulders,
And bringing order to the mess my father was,
I was sad more than detesting growing up to be an adult,
Much like my parents, fighting all day long,
I wanted an end to the sadness in my father's eyes,
And I hurt myself for reasons not known to me back then,
But my father had read me like all fathers do,
I lived my entire life without any dream,
Snubbed by the world like a lost mendicant,
Not that I had any desire to be noticed,
Many years and miles my parents left me,
And left clues that I began to unravel late in life,
I was still single but there was a dream emerging,
It felt so right and something my soul yearned for,
I wanted to dig in just for the love of it,

I wanted to contribute my part to the world,
It is indeed a dream,
And it will lead me till the very end.

9. HOMAGE TO THE WHEELS

See those clean-shaven monks,
They dream of salvation,
Renouncing all but themselves,
For them 'I' is a dream,
For even an ant craves for a name,
And it must not stop much like us,
For a dream is an illusion,
It is there to make life a living,
To make worthless men push their limits,
Until they cave in and can see the foolishness of the skies,
Some go beyond what they presumed would be,
As they struggle to recollect their starting point,
Some dream of the evening,
When they can bounce out of a working day,
For them a dream is not their own,
Many lives are scripted with their help,
Most of those lives shall betray and refuse a dirge,
When the altruistic is finally gone,
If ever I had the time for a dream,
It would take me to a snowy land,
Where I would hold hands of my beloved,
And live with my parents forever,
But the dog barks and the traffic snoozes,
In a perturbed normal day,

And I watch some new faces, confused and hungry,
Trying to postulate life in a single day,
They have young dreams,
Little do they know,
That a dream unfulfilled is actually a dream fulfilled.

10. THE HIGHEST DREAM

Love is the highest dream,
It is dry desert land of pricks and stones,
It has fire and venom for a lost wanderer,
It lasts longer than a mountain needs to form,
It has not been tried ever before,
People of the valley have been hurt enough,
To venture into the impossible, far from their oasis,
Do not come near, the sign reads,
If not the venom, the darkness shall kill you,
Love is a word most spoken of but hardly spoken,
For men will hide what is beyond them,
And not talk about it in matters of immediate attention,
Each eye lies,
Each breath is taken with incompleteness,
We rub over the mundane,
But our hands and hearts speak some other language,
We have learnt to hide our soul,
And we talk about the wonderful thing called 'dream',
A million ages hence the valley will nod,
To the same sounds carrying the same dilemma,
Of life and its rainbow of dreams,
Each one accomplished yet still not enough,
For a dream is where the angels tread,
With a halo of love and a lesson for all,

To love our brothers and sisters until we depart.

11. PURE DREAM

Dreams are born out of bosoms of unfairness,
When a human wears the cloak of a human,
When the daggers cease and there do rise,
A dream that needs no pennies,
A man and his voice echo a hidden dream,
That is accomplished way before the storm,
Count your blessing if you are hard done by,
If someone is a colossal of unfairness,
If your life had been snatched away too soon,
Don't raise no flags or dissent,
Cry you may but in heedless tears,
A dream is not a fashion statement,
It is the right and heart of each human being,
And we shall have it at all cost,
It lies hidden in our core during our struggles,
Don't give up now and run away,
Someone wants to carve you and pass the buck,
To the evil that deliberately created chaos in others' lives,
For them the gates have already opened,
To a place deep below existence,
Pure dreams are meant to come true,
They are with that woman and man,
That are slaves to the master,
But are special guests to the Almighty,
Like Lord Jesus washing the feet of his disciples,

Dreams are for those with a purpose,
To lend a helping shoulder to the needy,
Not caring about their own blood-stained linen,
Yes, I do have a dream,
And I shall until the day I die.

12. COME AS YOU MAY

I left my home deep among the mountains,
To walk the land empty handed,
Like a curse on me to wake up to reality,
That has men and women corrupt to the neck,
Where every little voice is unheard and crushed,
Where lies and deceit make up the filth in the city,
Where the roads are a mile long for the greater privileged,
Where the one sought for has a caravan wherever he goes,
Lest he may be inflicted by some germ of sneeze,
While poor men walk in the boiling heat on broken streets,
To succumb to an empty stomach and faint to die,
When no one comes to claim their body,
And they are shoved into the local cremation ground,
In this land did anyone have a dream,
Do not elicit the wrath of the Almighty,
For His ways show no mercy,
That damp bag lying in that far away cell,
Can feed millions,
Time is running out, O! felicitated,
Let dreams take rest,
We need to see the hidden faces of the populace,
For God always provides to the one that deserve,
And no good man ever sleeps without food,
Justice takes time but is done eventually,
Progress is a tale for that hardworking man,

Who does not sleep for the sake of his own people,
Dreams are the flowers of transcendence,
It is not the individual but the divine that dreams,
Resting the weight of this world on able shoulders,
Let's not give up our struggle,
For the good shall never die.

13. THE DAY SHALL ARRIVE

If only we were allowed to see,
Not hustle at the bell of a thought,
If we could tear off the cloak of darkness we are in,
Vanity and conceit the twin sisters of havoc,
Yet nothing fails us if we should know,
Each day is an event to the close,
Of a long running drama,
In which each one regardless has to play a part,
Don't be sad if dreams are lost along the way,
You were young once with a pocket of dreams,
Late in the day they were all gone,
As each one felt the fatigue of age,
When the mind could not spring an idea,
When the master failed to lead,
When the mind did not take off,
When you realized that the dreams you dreamt,
Way back of landing on the moon,
Didn't mean anything even after its accomplishment,
It did not make you stand apart from the rest,
But you have to lie and falsely claim,
That which did not happen,
The birds are twittering unabated,
They just like to indulge in their usual games,
Ten thousand years from now,

You may hear the same birds,
But by then you would have unravelled,
The mysteries of birth and life,
And cast yourself aloof from the commoners,
To become the odd one out,
And shall work on a magnificent dream,
And lend your heart and soul for your people,
But today you must accept your atheism,
And walk by quietly,
For the vagaries of ignorance and the 'fall' leads to wisdom,
And that dawn is the greatest in our lives,
When we find ourselves.

14. TRUE LOVE

I dreamt a dream of red and pink,
Of snow and tenderness of a flower,
I thought fairy tales do exist and come true,
I dreamt of a queen on her throne of bright,
To place herself in my heart,
But God denied that purple snowy winter,
I walked to pillar and post searching,
She was nowhere to be found,
I was often reminded of my bland skin colour,
And that a princess of snow is meant for white skin,
But my heart was pure and bright as dawn,
I never gave up hope like my father,
Then in the low light of twilight,
I found a princess on a carriage coming my way,
She passed me by to the mountains of glory,
She said she shall wait for me,
My heart knew no bounds of immense happiness,
I danced along for the remaining days here on earth,
Love is the greatest dream of all,
Every man and woman have been gifted,
With true love,
If only they could know.

15. YOUR WISH

The Lord said, 'Dream a dream, if you may…',
Some opted for rockets, some bags of gold, some beauty,
Some wanted palaces, some wanted to leave their homes,
Some wanted lovers, some wanted freedom, some wanted professions,
The Lord quickly made a list,
And each one got exactly what they wanted,
But there arose a box of disease with the gifts,
A million problems that never seemed to end,
Like a room full of mosquitoes and that shining sword,
Could only deal with a few,
Their minds never ceased to think random thoughts,
Where one thought had a life of a day at least,
Their dreams lacked purity and made them very sick,
Their dreams became their nemesis, to the point of complete ruin,
'That is all you can get in one life, children', the Lord said,
The people clapped for their success,
While their inner cried,
They denied the Hands of the Giver,
Their wealth was indeed their own creation,
Their rise to the peak of success was a result of hard labour,
And not some God of stone,
The time arrived then to leave this world,
They looked back at their life,
Their cheating, lies and corrupt ways flashed one by one,
As their throats ran dry like a thirst of ages,

Something was missing somewhere,
Before a crowd of people that stood,
Around their body in a hospital,
They passed away and the moaning began.

16. DREAMS AND CAGES

Let your dreams fly,
And not be bound in a cage of slavery,
For slaves are never born free,
Hold the wind in peaceful waters,
In a ship that leads you to a land of dreams,
Where laughter and rest are in abundance,
Where the battle of life is done,
And you rejoice in triumph,
Then you live for a million years,
In a life of fifty,
Where being alone is best company,
And you don't need those eyes of wobble,
That brim with thoughts unbecoming,
Of a kind and peaceful human,
Dreams are the butterflies in a green meadow,
With soft grass and brilliant flowers,
Glowing in an ocean of sunshine,
Where you can pick on dreams till noon,
For some cold water and tea back in shade,
When the sun starts to burn the skin,
Life is the most beautiful thing given,
And dreams are like colours on a white canvas,
We can create infinite patterns and shapes,
For we have skills hidden in all of us,

You need just two hands,
And a curious mind,
Let God play with us,
With riddles and puzzles,
As Santa comes along with a bag of dreams,
Each winter in his red dress,
Telling all that life is nothing but a joke,
That some have taken too seriously,
Let every moment be a dream,
Let it flow freely,
Small one and big ones,
And we shall all leave a mark,
Before heading high above the skies.

17. PARDON ME

There are people that shall sacrifice,
Their lives for others,
The truest lovers they say,
Never met,
The man young and handsome,
Is a man full of dreams,
For his people and for himself,
There's his lover that met him long ago,
She's sitting in one corner wondering,
If he still remembers her,
But the man is on a rocket,
He's got a girl by his side,
He's got woman at his beck and call,
For no one saw a more desirable man,
He responds with affirmation,
Never wasting a day on his flight to the moon,
His parents soon prepare for his wedding,
To a wealthy girl for that is what he desired,
That lost lover of ages is sick and dying,
Her lips shall not reveal what's in her heart,
With the name of her lover etched on it,
She is a spinster no one wants to have,
Life is not a bouquet of dreams,
Where the flowers in it bloom endlessly,
This is a cruel world,

Where no one knows what sorrow they cause,
To someone that is ready to toss their lives,
Into the fire and burn to ashes,
But each man has to account for,
The damage caused to someone,
That did not matter ever in their flight of dreams,
What are these dreams then,
Just garbage,
Don't cry O! angel,
God will do justice.

18. A GREATER DREAM

We have a dream,
When the world is kinder towards women,
When the old ones are worth gold,
When little children are not forced to beg,
When students sweat in peace to learn,
And have deep respect for teachers,
When humanity is willing to sacrifice for evolution,
When the world realizes that there is no 'greatness',
And that we all fit that label,
When our hearts can feel the pain of others,
And give to others what we can when required,
When science and art work for a better world,
That is beautiful and brings greater peace,
And take people to the depths of human imagination,
When the dark cloud that is over us has disappeared,
And every human is truly free,
When we respect and adore our ancestors,
And gather the immense wisdom of the previous ages,
When honesty and truth are a way of life,
True to the naivety of a little child,
When the world travels at the speed of light,
When guns and cannons and nuclear bombs,
Missiles, rockets and army tanks,
Become anachronistic and an artefact for museums,
Don't wake me up too soon,

For there is a kink somewhere,
And it's turned out to be the fatal leak,
My dreams are still similar to many other dreams,
Don't dream just dreams,
Take humanity with you,
Then you would have served your people,
Until then let the scare not defeat you,
Try and face the odds,
Let time come up with the answers,
It has always acted as a balm on torn hearts,
Dream your dream, then, whatever that may be.

19. O! LOVE

'I want to be famous,
A young man from England said,
Says he is the son of poor father,
Who could not afford a new dress,
For himself and his wife on special days,
They barely had enough on their plate either,
Many a times the father drank and ate,
Off the morning air and evening mist,
The boy never came home one night,
And his father let him go,
And so did his mother off their minds,
Never to see him again without any complaints,
That boy in twenty years,
Was much talked about in England and elsewhere,
He had turned a billionaire,
His father stuck his eyes on the T.V. one night,
In the market place,
He saw his son waving to the crowds,
He quietly walked back to his bed,
And pulled on his sheets to shut eyes,
He knew someone would knock at his door soon,
The next morning, a young lad in the finest suit,
Walked into the old man's house,
Father and son were happy to see each other,
Very soon the family had their own bungalow,

Down the poshest street in London,
They did live happily from that time onwards,
Before dying father called his son to his room,
'Son, I did not thank you enough for what you have done for us,
'My heart just weeps to imagine your great struggle,
'My son I have something to tell you,
'Love is a tender word,
'It is expressed very softly,
'Only your soul can hear it,
'But it makes a man complete,
'It is missed by most in this world,
'Including me,
'Being famous is a good thing,
'Money does bring happiness,
'But it lasts only for a while,
'But if you have missed that tender word called 'love',
'Then there is no way you can hear it,
'In the remaining days of your life,
'I am leaving, my son,
'I am proud of you,
'But please, think of what I just said,
'This suit on me is perhaps the last one I shall wear,
'Take care, my son,
'I love you very much.

20. WHAT A DREAM

I dream of a snowy land,
At the feet of my dear parents,
In complete silence and peace,
With my woman by my side,
Resting and peaceful after the mindless storm,
As we live together each day,
And a make it a day to remember,
With the log of fire burning softly,
In crackling sounds it does intervene,
The stove is hot over a blue flame,
It is as constant as the lone star in the skies,
The room is warm and yellow lights,
Wash the room with a mellow delight,
My woman is helping Momma in the kitchen,
And Papa is quiet with the pages of a book,
His glasses are hanging loose over his nose bridge,
He looks at me sometimes after a few lines,
And he shuts the book and pulls his reading glasses,
And looks pensive wanting to share something,
I look into his eyes but we don't speak,
Soon we hear sounds of laughter,
From among the ladies followed by the men,
Soon Papa breaks into a new thought,
That he likes to share with me,
And the ladies too join in,

Listening very carefully,
The thought seems to the birth of an idea,
It is a noble idea and we all agree,
We have some soft music,
And couples dance in the small living room,
To dim lights,
It's the favourite tune of my beloved,
Days are spent thus,
In total gay abandon,
What more can I dream of.

PART TWO

21. DOG PATHOS

I saw my whistling master,
Like a poke at my giggling bone,
While that last swat of cane failed to register,
Quite unjust when I was trying to be my own.
I sit all day when my master is gone,
He feeds me to the tick of a clock,
My bowel wants to empty its stuff on the lawn,
But my master wants a clean lawn in his walk.
It's not entirely my fault to be caned,
What do I do if my stomach is impudent,
I don't blame my master and my great pain,
Just meet me when I cry to a lonely repent.

22. CARRIAGE OF CONCEIT

Carriage of conceit was devoid of the charioteer,
The horses with blinkers trotted on their shoes,
The day was bright on a day of the cold winter,
The big wheels rolled with the carriage on the news.
The passengers were hidden behind curtains,
The often peeked into the bright day outside,
Within it was warm with pouring sweat like rain,
The horses were headed somewhere to recover lost pride.
The night fell too soon than suspected,
The passengers heard no cheer outside,
The horses did tire and the huge wheels deflated,
Until late in the night the distinguished died.

23. WHO HAS GOT IT

The world is curious,
Who's got the key,
Perhaps with hot movie stars so mysterious,
Or the vermilion monk with words of peace.
People join in with joints between fingers,
Ready to adopt the popular culture,
With the rich ones do they linger,
Closer to Nirvana, a rich man's capture.
But the rich ones know,
Stifled and incomplete do they feel,
That they might have missed a bow,
Miserable and alone on costly wheels.

24. WAIT FOR THE SHIP

Wait for the ship if you can,
It is stuck midway on the sea,
Look its hoots have a limited span,
Don't hurry if you hear someone plea.
Life is not a potion to guzzle too soon,
Life is like a still wind locked in time,
Life cannot be lived in a shoe box of gloom,
To pin one's eyes on women and wine.
Millions walk the street I see,
With scared eyes and tortured limbs,
Roaming aimlessly from twenty to eighty,
What happened to the longing for a glimpse.

25. GO TO MOTHER

When grief takes a heavy toll,
Of lost dreams and eyes of sorrow,
When you are lost like a fish in a bowl,
Go to Mother the day before 'morrow.
Speak what's in your heart or be silent,
For Mother knows you and your pain,
She will show you light if you are patient,
If your love is true and not fixed on gains.
You are Her beloved son,
You have a place above the skies,
Mother shall tell you what has to be done,
It's been long since someone walked by.

26. GREAT MEN

There came the great men,
That gave us the wheel and the airplane,
Bridges, and light bulbs and knowledge hidden,
Stretching limits of human progress through their pain.
What did you leave for yourself, Sirs,
A heart of lament for the one you love,
That did not come even in your blur,
Of a new age dawning before the rest above.
Selfless and giving as you are,
Perhaps losing sleep for something unheard,
While the rest sleep in peace too far,
From the struggle and the elusive word.

27. A TOUCH AWAY

We are a touch away from darkness,
It's almost twilight and people are rushing homewards,
The distance is still visible and so is kindness,
Minds have begun to worship fake stalwarts.
The hands are falling into the treasure chest,
That has loads of golds and silver,
The makers have backed off and taken off their vest,
The eyes look for perfection in every corner.
The pied piper is back again,
He's drawing people with his charm,
Geeks are locked away in disdain,
Urging, 'we need the darkness before the storm.

28. A MORNING FEAST

The sun is about to rise to end darkness,
The sky is pink and purple with a soft touch,
The grass is a sea of pearls like washed tress,
The feeling of stillness and inner peace such.
The birds have begun to stretch and move,
They have found this lawn for a visit,
I push my kettle of water for tea to brew,
My dog is restless to unleash and fly as a bullet.
The people are awake after last night's nightmares,
Life now is simple with no danger,
Like a new world has arisen, sinless and fair,
Before the night of past comes again so ginger.

29. BEFORE YOU LEAVE

Leave a trace before you leave,
For the lady sunshine of your heart,
She has been waiting beyond your honest sleeve,
Don't you feel empty with your trophies apart.
Don't look at the name of the poet,
Or from where the words come from,
Just sink into the meaning before your list of regrets,
Isn't it too late in the day to roam.
Some things are meant to be, though,
There's nothing one can do,
But the magic is in the heart of gold,
And it brings lost travellers home soon.

30. IT TAKES GOOD

Goodness has become a disease,
We are better off with the eternal slip,
Don't even look at fire of peace,
You will be saved of the monster trip.
Burnt faces and bodies have eyes of hope,
Suddenly after the storms of youth,
By old age they did learn the ropes,
When life introduced a new person of missing tooth.
Look at these people walking by,
Too sacred to risk and truly unholy,
Living in illusion and camouflaged by lies,
Good is not an option for a culture of willy-nilly.

31. THE CLASSIC

They were the classic family,
With outreaching hands of salvation,
It's a dreaded way of life of calamity,
Within an ocean of mediocrity and degradation.
Esteemed members were rich shadows from the past,
Locked and enslaved like sinners,
In a land inhospitable yet chaste,
With poverty undefined, a homeless spinner.
Life not a piece of cake, the old man says,
You bring what you do,
The past is a mirror for living days,
When we sum up and leave this zoo.

32. ROMEO AND JULIET

There was in Rome,
The greatest love story of our times,
Romeo and Juliet died in love forlorn,
Montecchio and Capulet didn't spare a dime,
For each one's blood and end,
The friar and his plot did the trick,
When Juliet faked her death and sent,
The message to Romeo that she had licked,
When Romeo did take his life first,
Followed by Juliet to end the feud,
While the families regretted for the hurt,
To two innocent children of history blurred.

33. UNEASE

Name a man not at unease,
And God shall,
People flee to a different country,
To escape the constant brawl.
And the limitless struggle in their land of birth,
But they too feel the unease,
For what their life's worth,
No one knows the ways of the breeze.
They fear that all will end one day,
And they shall without a penny or a pin,
Life is exactly what they lived, they say,
And nothing more than a worthless spin.

34. UNABASHED

You are looking for gold and silver,
When there's plenty around you,
One that shall last forever,
But you are blind and crippled too.
Give a piece of bread to a poor man,
And God shall bless you for good,
Someone with hunger of days cannot stand,
When no helping hand would,
Be kind towards him,
Your stacks are overflowing with cash,
You the rich for your future of grim,
What happened to the present, you walk unabashed.

35. PEACE AND BREAD

We got lost in the valley of death,
Where the end was imminent in the moment,
Two hearts in love for what it is worth,
Shall never meet or repent,
For we are seekers of peace and bread,
Another way shall lead to another day,
With a load on our shoulders of other instead,
We do what we are told and dare not disobey,
We have won peace and bread,
In appalling speed and perks to boot,
All alone in a villa we sit like the dead,
For the peace flew away and with it the loot.

36. UNSEEN

Our world contains people around us,
That happened to be a part of our lives,
Therein lies the clue to our happiness,
And not some distant star newly arrived.
Don't ask for the path of peace,
Or how are we supposed to get along,
Know that even Buddha does not hold the keys,
Humanity is a mass of excuses for wrongs,
They say this time will not come again,
All this while you have been roaming in darkness,
For someone to light the candle like business gains,
And you flutter away in all politeness.

37. WHY DO YOU

O! bird of delight,
Singer in the woods,
Why do you sing at such height,
On tree branches where no one could,
Hear your song,
Why do you sing at all,
Each passing day your beak so wrong,
For haven't you heard the nightingale for salt,
I sing for it delights me,
And makes my heart lighter,
For the hole in my chest make me stymied,
To live in peace and inspire that occasional writer.

38. HANG AROUND

Hang around for the coffee,
Don't busy your hands too much,
Sit in silence to know your role in the movie,
It's the movie of life and we must be without any crutch.
The mind lag needs careful construction,
One wrong step and we are booked again,
Be ready to burn the mind and body in succession,
It's a delicate affair that usually ends in vain.
You don't need to be in history,
Or have an auspicious pedigree,
All you need is elementary,
Yet one hardly witnessed that lush tree.

39. CANDY KIDS

Candy kids are the ones with silver spoon,
They frolic in a garden of fulfilled desire,
Seldom do they walk out of their golden cocoon,
In a world of poverty and inhospitable mire,
They don't need to speak or utter a word,
When followed by legions of paparazzi,
It's enough to be the offspring of the revered,
It's a dive into comfort and be lazy.
The candy kids are above existence,
They have what people spend their lives searching,
And never reach the state of abundance,
Candy kids know not the calamity of living.

40. NOMINATION

The following 21 poems were nominated for the Emily Dickinson Award 2024.

41. WHAT IS WAR

War is a flea in the mind of the enemy,
It happens without any reason at all,
Like the one in a complete family,
When the one at fault is hard to call,
And one offspring is bound to fall off the tree.
Who needs guns and cannons and missiles,
When the matter could end with a cup of tea and
biscuits,
As the evening falls and each have walked a
mile,
When the trouble makers were asked to sit,
And drown their egos and the disputed file.
Let the guns be gone and children play,
For a glimpse of tomorrow if only left alive,
War is a waste when the stricken families pray,
It is but a vent to great conceit on which nations
thrive,
It is the wind and is here to stay.

42. ANATOMY OF BUSINESS

In the lighter vane the grass has grown,
And some birds now fly higher than before,
As humans will lie and mask their own,
Hear a sudden rush from critters and more,
To be a human and far from an emotionless
stone.
We need more than a plate of food,
We need palaces and an army of workmen,
For enough is not quite enough where we stood,
We must amass and plunder for progress and our
ken,
No one can get over the worldly brood.
Every man and woman in their rising stress,
Money no good and the mind suffering,
Find no end to the loud siren of mess,
A dull day and fingers of blame in a bullring,
Crashing and smashing in a silent regress.
Look at the fleet of cars and the quiet palace,
What is missing is the flight on gossamer
strings,
One life and a lack of grace,
What shall bring with the bite and the sting,
The fits of argument gone like smoke of waste.

43. POT OF FUN

The bees with their sweet tongue,
Circle around flowers at hems,
Of gardens lit by the bright sun,
The ants know not how to stem,
Their abundant flow on barrels of guns.
The dogs got a sniff,
Its happiness and gaiety hidden in its legs,
Sleeps all day and eats the meat stiff,
The moth and the butterfly need not beg,
Their freedom from fingers is no age-old myth.
The squirrels have hefty backs,
The dote on the nut with levered teeth,
Bushy tails they do not fit in traps,
The lofty birds have a home above the heath,
They feed on less on a road without a map.
Humans sulk and cry and moan,
With a brain to manage they forget the pot,
With an evil intent and a heart of stone,
They push and plunder and miss the plot,
The pot of fun is left undone.

44. MY LOVER

They say marriage is hell,
Women want more than babies,
Hence, I saved the sinful bell,
Now middle aged and heavy,
My spirits brightest and no offspring to tell.
Crazy as I am there roamed a vision,
For I do believe in God,
It smiled for years on end with precision,
Also, at the mortuary with mother on her bed,
None revealed of the girl of His creation.
She dazzles when I peep behind my eyes,
Like frozen in time, a little mischievous,
With bob hair lips of sighs,
Mysterious, she makes me nervous,
For if I tie the knot with some other right?

45. WHY ARE WE LIVING

Why is the butterfly winging,
Why don't snails give up,
Why do birds leave the nest, wandering,
Why are those ants out of luck,
Being crushed to death a ringing.
Why does the day break every day,
As we hustle and muscle for something,
We cry out for matters beyond and foray,
When what we need is lost in a blink,
While the lover chases love to be gay.
There's a toast of wife and kids,
That become a burden in the passing day,
Marriage devoid of love as the lovers bid,
In all fakeness they choose to stay,
While love vanishes as if it did exist.

46. PICTURE Ms. RANDALL

Picture Ms. Randall,
She's crossed her hands low,
Big boys can afford a scandal,
As she stands in a sari with pedicured toes,
She's so white with a soft marble glow.
Some heathen eyes give her dirty looks,
She can't find the one for her,
The crowd of eyes and this stolen brook,
Can not the moment spur,
The brave one out of a fairy book.
For love happens without a sound,
And Ms. Randal is caught,
Between the loaf and coffee rounds,
The staff room of Senior high she sought,
Looks bare with just the hound,
Of loneliness and the missing plot.

47. PENNI WORTH A PENNY

Penni is worth a penny,
He walks on barren roads,
Under the hot sun or when rainy,
He knows not about the heavy load,
He carries with no sound as a pony.
Penni wonders about those eyes,
That he never saw in years,
Like none were to answer his sighs,
His heavy eyes washed in tears,
In a world where everyone lies.
Penni lived through tough times,
His own making,
For that is his constant crime,
He knows not his actions or forsaking,
His own being for no rhyme,
Or reason until the sound of him breaking,
When he found her in her prime,
And he chose to walk like a student abiding.

48. LEAVES OF LOVE

Leaves of love often bitter,
They grow in the wild few,
Trample them by foot and the lose their glitter,
Till the time you finish your stew,
On a bright new day after the night saunter.
When did it happen your memory fails,
That woman or man in reams of veil,
Like love that just happens in no gust or gale,
Woman as far as that man like a seed that is
sealed,
Will offer that last chance and if you fail...
Many then happened to come and go,
The man and his tryst with flesh,
While the woman felt a chivalrous bow,
The man and his lost love in the great rush,
While the woman with a different loyalty low.
What happened thus is for all of us to know.

49. WHAT IS THIS CREED

What is this new creed,
Where did the song go,
What is this sunken breed,
Them eyes and the lost bow,
Hear them sing in broken tweed.
A world with a lost rhythm,
A melody that will not appear,
With a semblance of the golden hymns,
Not long ago a song sung softly and sincere,
Of times when alone with tapping limbs,
Of lonesome feathers and no one near.
Catch the one you are looking for,
Don't dangle and amble around the bush,
Gather forces with 'I love you' at her door,
Stay with her and do not rush,
Grow and live each day in days of sore,
Then paint a melody with the hardened brush,
You are but a sapling of our fathers that tore,
Their very being in a long hush.

50. WHAT IS THE FUSS

Jonathan got a new car,
He's looking into the map,
Kimberly finally got seven zeroes after the bar,
She'd be flying first class above the air gap,
She owns a cottage above the hill far.
Emanuel has got power as the head,
Of a unit he has command over a team,
He is busy signing papers he hasn't read,
He yawns in the morning over cups of milk
seams,
Men bow low before him indeed.
We need money for an easy ride,
In pristine places and unmatched comfort,
For sumptuous food and five-star nights,
We break our backs for that dazzling port,
When going through it doesn't seem right.
We must hear the good sage again,
Hunger for power, money and comfort,
Are all a waste in a corrupt vein,
Love we must seek from the heart,
We then won't feel like an expanding balloon,
That must bulge till the sound of a dart.

51. A PLACE CALLED HEAVEN

What did you hear child,
Your heart is the black devil,
It urges you to cross over the mild,
And drown in the thick froth of hell,
To see you perish and leave your spoil.
Why did you emerge my child,
When you were put to sleep,
The world is a treacherous guile,
When you are pushed by uptight creeps,
To last in the queue of proven gentile.
The war will never end my child,
It reaches small peaks now and again,
Until you forget your name in the pile,
Or where you are headed insane,
The picture will never emerge my child,
You were discarded for your sin,
Go away you poor lad.

52. A SCHOOLBOY LOVE

Madam Tuss punished little Tim,
For an incomplete homework,
Bright eyes, bob hair, tall and trim,
Lips of red thin of complaints and the works,
Tim looks the other way with a face so grim,
As Tuss talks to Tim's parents for the hidden spark.
Tuss in thoughts she knows not why,
Her life slipping away too soon,
A grown-up woman with matters beyond the skies,
A cheerful face for all to swoon,
She dazzles yet broken within too many times.
Soon to be betrothed,
To a man she does not love,
A sad tale she has a baby before being tethered,
A compromise she has dreams of her dove,
Who will save her or be bothered.
Tim the little one,
Has matters that must be dealt with,
He likes Madam Tuss in spite of her tongue,
The scary habit of loving hate without a stitch,
He runs away into his upper rung,
Forgetting about Tuss in the growing screech.

53. HERITAGE OF MAN

I have a house by the river,
The river has cold water in spring,
I live in a small house by the boulders,
A wife and two children I did bring,
I left my mother and went back never.
I have a job in the Carton rail,
They make me work night and day,
I wave my flags to see the cargo sail,
My children grew up in the sun and hay,
I love my wife and kids like the holy grail.
My life and those hermits I see,
They have walked alone far and wide,
Their lives are unreal far from the melee,
What do they have if not a blushing bride,
They never touch women for the earthly spree,
I cannot see what they do if not provide,
Can we live like them within the family tree.

54. BAG OF SORROW

He walked with a heavy load of sorrow,
His shoulders too heavy and bent,
Shades of a rainbow tomorrow,
Did they show for worthwhile spent,
On butter crusted groves for the morose.
He walked with his eyes shut,
He walked at his own risk for so long,
There was no end around the holy hut,
You tired soul did you hear the gong,
If not then where to the strut.
There is no place to go to,
You have been walking for too long,
Without a name or hands with the stew,
You lover perhaps and her song,
You live in unreal and mingle with the rubbish
hue,
You know not where the world has sprung.
When will your day arrive,
It is getting very late now,
You better sail away than be alive,
For before a million you did bow,
And God does not contrive,
For someone to hold the sea so low,
For so long and strive,
Until pulled in from a wrecked boat.

55. THESE ARE THE DAYS

Breeze of satin over weary skin,
Where has the world been,
Velvet of colors on flowers akin,
To a moment in paradise unseen,
Gifts of solitude and the world's in spin.
Come to the earth my stricken brethren,
There you will find peace,
In your oblong frame of ivy and sin,
Bury the hatchet with a touch of grease,
You shall carry no mountains or gin
When you leave forever unease.
Flowers are waiting for a touch,
The leaves have dropped their heads,
The garden is still twittering such,
For smiles and cheer from hands of bread,
That have found the meadow in their search.

56. VANDERDICT

Vander was an addict,
To women on the evening street,
To smoke under a pale sky unlit,
To heavy water of spirit,
To nights of high atop the summit.
Vander and his wife and kids,
Rushes to office in his senses,
Lying by night the way he did,
His wife with dusty lenses,
Let him go long ago for the kids.
Vander and his gurgling mind,
Like boiling water and its bubbles,
Ready to blow off heat with one Ms. Rosand,
His wife is aware but still on the double,
She rummaged her boxes for a lost husband,
The ring of promises when she was single.
The wife holds on in spite of it all,
She vows never to leave her husband,
Even when the temptress is on call,
To their very home with shoes of sand,
As she sits in a corner all night against the wall.

57. A FATHER AND SON

The father had seen it all,
The son and his haphazard motion,
Calling for injury at beck and call,
'Do not try to swallow the ocean,
'Call it off, sainthood is beyon
'I shall leave if you pursue,
'I can't see my boy so bruised or gone,
'I have never seen someone so blue,
'You have my heart so forlorn,
'Take that leap if there's no clue,
'I shall wait for you till dawn.d all.
'Do not try to walk that road,
'The age is not right O! wasted earth,
'They'll kill you and take your abode,
'It's not in the unconscious by birth,
'To open their eyes and not hoard,
'That satchel of truth for its worth.

58. WHAT IS IT

A child was born in the summer,
It could walk and speak like all else,
The God's above and imminent matters,
No one to hinder their daisies and dales,
That child with skies of dust and tatters.
Those men and women speak so low,
Their faces with smiles that don't go deep,
Robbed of the sense of bow,
Or love for the shepherd and its sheep,
Carrying venom in spits they sow,
Seeds of hinder for a heartless reap,
To someone soft like grass of mow.
God the saviour of people,
That know not about their foe,
And are sucked into plans lethal,
When someone calls in tears or so,
And gives of himself to the final bugle,
God comes to save them in sorrow,
For the pain too high in the endless struggle.

59. I'D RATHER BE

I'd rather be a husband with no wife,
A father with no children,
A sailor on a sea of strife,
For those moments of no hindrance,
Alone in a torn battlefield rife,
With blood of demons of encumbrance.
For the end is what matters,
The road passed by does not exist,
Those fetters so strong around haters,
Or those that persist,
In denying the Holy and a power greater,
Soul of rubber they all insist.
I'd rather die than open my eyes,
To find the world locked in a box,
With no light but frustration and sighs,
When with a small flame they could knock,
At the doors with no disguise,
And realize the unwanted lock,
That should have been broken for the skies,
Finally, to open eyes and promptly knock,
At those Doors of the meek and wise.

60. OVERCROWDED PARK

Motley of faces have come to the park,
Where every man and woman are royal,
Picture the native as they hark,
From strangers of faraway soil,
Taking vows to defend their lark.
Go home you stranger of another land,
We have problems of our own,
That does not need your stand,
For these are from the seeds sown,
Long ago by preachers of this land.
Home is where the heart is,
It needs you if you can understand,
Your path is wavered and amiss,
Live till you grow sick and bland,
Life's too short for a kiss,
Of a world that you left behind.

61. WHAT IS LOST

Dominic wrote until his last,
Verses that did not catch the eye,
Of the kings of kingdoms vast,
Or of the public and passerby,
He questioned himself at last.
Dominic and his appointed day,
When the path was decided long ago,
Now the time to walk and say,
It was a good life amidst the raging row,
For words silent as the hiss of hay.
So long the people of a lovely land,
Breathe in art and create your piece,
In need no crowd or an auspicious hand,
Let the blood in your veins never cease,
To flow and dissolve in a silvery band.

www.ingramcontent.com/pod-product-compliance
Lightning Source LLC
LaVergne TN
LVHW041133150826
845673LV00007B/2306

9798896102380